JOHN HUDSON is an award winning poet. Among his previous poetry publications are *Medusa Muse* (Abbey Hill, 1996), *The Pumpkin Lantern, Selected Poems 1985–2003* (Markings, 2007), *Star Wood Stone* (Glasgow Botanic Gardens, 2000), *Garden Of Love, Poems in English and French* (Wider Eye, 2009) and *Shed* (E17 Arts Festival, 2011). He is also editor of *Round About Burns* (Dumfries and Galloway Libraries, 1996) and *The Collected Poems of William Nicholson* (GC Books, 1999). Between 1995 and 2010, he edited the literary magazine *Markings*. He has twice been the recipient of a Scottish Arts Council Writers Bursary and various travel bursaries and residency awards. John was born in London but now lives in Galloway, Scotland.

Its economy is striking, vivid images conjured up in just a few words; the commonplace in counterpoint to the uncommon; well-worn figures of speech shining with new meaning; the profound rubbing up against the everyday and, in the process, teasing out unconsidered layers of meaning.

LIZ THOMSON, BookBrunch

I liked the underpinning rhythmic drive, the subtle half-rhymes, and the thought-provoking wit tinged with occasional sensuous/sensual imagery ... the referencing to other cultures and belief-systems. You have got a winner of a collection there.

ROGER ELKIN, former editor of *Envoi* magazine

ONLINE RESOURCES

More information on John Hudson plus a complete reading guide and study aid for Earth, designed for the general reader, teachers and students can be found at www.johnhudson.info.

Earth

JOHN HUDSON

Luath Press Limited
EDINBURGH
www.luath.co.uk

First published 2012

ISBN: 978-1-908373-36-6

The paper used in this book is recyclable. It is made
from low chlorine pulps produced in a low energy, low emissions
manner from renewable forests.

Typeset in 10.5 point Sabon by
3btype.com

The author's right to be identified as author of this work under the
Copyright, Designs and Patents Act 1988 has been asserted.

Text © John Hudson 2012

Acknowledgements

THE AUTHOR WOULD like to thank the Scottish Arts Council, now Creative Scotland, for its generous support in the form of a bursary to assist in the completion of this book, and Shetland Arts which supported a residency in 2009 during which some of the poems in *Earth* were written.

No collection of poems is ever completed without the caring and careful advice of friends and family. *Earth* is no exception. I'd like to thank everyone who has played their part in bringing this work to publication.

Burns Night 2009 previously appeared in *Adrian, Scotland Celebrates Adrian Mitchell* (Markings, Scotland 2009), and *The Eastern Empire* appeared in *For Angus* (Los Poetry Press, Cambridge 2009). *Elegy* formed part of an installation, *Fils d'Ecosse* that I built with artist Cyril Barrand for the French Institute, Edinburgh in June 2008. *Wester Voe* featured on BBC Radio Shetland and *After the Flood* on Alive Radio, Dumfries.

EARTH

Strange Birth

It is thundering
when you arrive –
not there, where you are
suddenly
gulping the world's air
to tears and laughter
but here, in France,
on an abandoned railway siding
by a water tower
with jasmine climbing
a rusty ladder to its empty top.

I walk with your shadow
around my ankles. The grey day
fades like a daguerreotype;
lightning flickers down florins on the path ahead.
Rain makes shoes rub raw my heels
as I dry the mobile,
re-read the news
that, suddenly, you are here.

May sunshine bless your days
may moonshine comfort your nights
may the oak tree keep you steadfast company
may the sea wash your eyes and keep them pure
may honey bees feed you
and nightingales sing you to sleep
may the stars give you wonder
and the planets be your guide
on all the paths you choose.

EARTH

It is thundering here
on the once-upon-a-time railway line
where navvies in photographs
proudly puff on clay pipes
and crinolined ladies ghost over the silvery footbridge
that today rots with rust;
it is thundering and the rain
is washing me away.
The path and I
wear each other's clothes.

But they say light turns gold
for remembrance and jubilation,
for spent journeys and those to come.
It is raging a storm
at the same time
you are born.

Earth

I, Earth, third rock from Sun,
hot stuff, fatal attraction,
Mister Magnetic,
surf gravity in a dicey embrace,
on a roll, a Salchow, wave-crest,
tumbling, never landing

I, Earth, ride Big Black
at three hundred K.P.S.,
spin on my axis day by giddy day
as my magma sambas,
continents curl a waltz
and my mountains star-jump –
meaning you, now,
in a break-dance, rolling every which way.

I, Earth, the real 24/7/365,
say hello,
open my leafy hand,
my cavernous heart.

EARTH

I'm nickel, iron, molten, mantle, plate
and a sliver of gas and mud
that sustains
Peter Hudd of St Andrews, Fife
who may
or may not
deserve his comfortable life.
(Who's judge? Not me.
What goes round comes round –
I'm proof of that)

I'm old,
some say venerable,
some crusty,
others vulnerable, in need of care –
it's my fifth billionth birthday soon –
but I'm up for make-overs,
keep fit and dress for special occasions,
notably funerals
where I'm always guest of honour.

I'm humus, loam, mixed with broken rock,
muck
to dig-over, plough and plant.
Some call me moody;
I prefer: seasonal.
I bud, blossom and fruit

into Earth's General Store,
Edmonton, Alberta, Canada:
more than a health food store –
a tool to achieve a healthier planet

EARTH

I'm down to earth –
realistic,
no frills, no fancy-pants flourishes, me:
straightforward, plain-talking, no-nonsense –
unlike Sis, Miss pose and pout,
hanging around the Bois du Boulogne,
glitz-gal, shameless show-off.
She breathes acid, burns
more than fingers;
her celestial body makes men stray.
Or my bro
with his gung-ho, ginger-nut, love-a-scrap ways.
That guy's got blood-lust in his DNA.
He's cold crazy to the bone and erratic with it,
a control-freak lording it over minor moons.
Small planets are like that.

To be fair, they say I'm earthy,
a bawd, lewd,
obsessed with procreation,
unspeakably crude,
not for polite company.

But there are other sides to Mister Blue.
I'm terracotta, earthenware,
museum stuff,
dainty delicate or durable
flasks, jars, cuneiforms, swastikas, bowls;
Linear, Beaker, Globular, Corded,
faience, majolica, Satsuma, Delft

EARTH

and porcelain,
Ming, Meissen, Wedgwood, Sèvres
the dukes and duchesses of a fine-dining spread,
so elegant, refined,
I hypnotise you,
impart, though I say it myself,
a strange, pervasive peace

I am sienna, ochre, umber
pigments slapped on stone: horses, bison, oryx,
and stickmen, shaman
tracking spoor,
running prey to earth

and the visionary:
terraforming,
terra nova...
Newfoundland,
Promised Land,
precious territory –
I've inspired religions, heavens-on-earth

I speak in tongues:
a terrir, to land,
return home,
llegar, to leave
on holiday, on business,
explorar,
make land,
give thanks,
kiss me,
kiss my grass

EARTH

Das Land, Der Erde
The Song of the Earth:
by strophe wistful, strong, awful, a furnace –
stour to dust, ashes to *asche*,
abschied,
back to Papa
or Mummy
whichever

I am an urn to hold you before the wind,
a wind to carry you across the ocean,
or a spade to plant your bones

I'm one of four elements in the ancient world,
with sisters air and water, brother fire
and one of five in China: Wu Xing,
with air, fire, water and wood my family

People ask, 'What on Earth?'
struck in amazement before a miracle,
see a pixie in their garden,
an angel by their bed –
not of this earth at all.
That's me

I'm your weatherman:
Earth Simulator, power-computer, world-beater.
I crunch digits like a shark bones in Yokohama, Japan,
dealing out zeros and ones,
on and off, hot and cold:
without me what would you talk about
on street corners, in shops, at work, over the 'phone?

EARTH

You spit on me,
plot, divide me up.
You fight over me, cut
me, drill me, poison me
as if you own me,
as if you can do with me as you please.
You could say you treat me like dirt.

Yet I love you.
When you've seen Big Black,
how planets, stars, even galaxies
are snuffed out,
no fault of their own,
by a wave of chance,
a ripple in the cosmic flux,
resentment and anger
aren't options.

And because there's nothing to forgive,
I'm unforgiving.

I'm even-handed, maintain zero potential.
I ground, absorb shocks, disperse calamity, dissolve voltage.
I balance, neutralise, make safe,
weather the storm, channel the bolt,
sky to earth,
as Zeus to his beloved Gaia –
babble, coo, mutter –
kabang!
It's all one to me.

EARTH

I am the vine that fuels the village hop,
hemlock to ease a poet's pain,
a day-dream, a dull Sunday afternoon
and your first kiss, lip to tender lip,
and its feisty follow-up
that brought you,
so innocent,
so selfish,
crying into this terrific, terrible world

I, Earth, am pity
even though you deem me pitiless

so spare a thought
for Earth, Lamb County, Texas, USA: a town,
eleven hundred souls, three hundred homes,
on the route between Plainview and Clovis,
slap bang twixt LA and Atlanta
hugging Interstate 70 and poor.

I am
a fox's lair.

Sacrifice

The young, blond girl from Egtved was buried
one summer day in 1370 BC.
National Museum of Denmark

Monday
she lay
on sphagnum and bog cotton,
closed her eyes,
to drift with the wind in the trees,
birdsong and buzzing bees.

On Tuesday, the lode of her body
sank.

Wednesday, she drank rain.
It fell and soaked her skin, her fingers,
hair, woollens, jewels, eyes, brain
and the cindered bones
of a child at her side

till, Thursday,
they became salt pickled in vinegar,
air-tight, untainted

and on Friday rose
to float in a glass casket,
be shared among
mothers and daughters

EARTH

as today's
peat and pollen grain,
hide and silence, wonder, gift,
bedtime story, sorrow, bread,

tomorrow's
earth.

Pilgrimage

The Natural world, in fact, enters us and becomes, well, becomes really a kind of life, it has a pilgrimage through us.
Peter Porter

A tractor blusters across the vineyard,
reaps harvest.
Like a sleepwalker
I settle in the garden lounger,
stare at the sun through a fringe on my pram,
hear the Morse of morning trains
rumbling from St James' Street to St Paul's.
There's a man in a suit and a wristwatch
with a *cantgetpastme* smile.

Dew settles, tubers take root,
honeysuckle scents the wayside
but who can see their insinuations
till way down the road?

At sunset a full moon
blanches fields into a white whale
that crests, dives and blows
toward the silver city.
Angoulême, like a fairy clipper coursing clouds,
explodes its sea-shell Gloria
scalloped white.

EARTH

The cathedral chimes,
diesel fumes drift on the breeze.
I sink beneath a shoal of mackerel
that flits like fleeting smiles
across the midnight sky.
Grapes in the hopper begin a slow decay,
split, drip and shrink
towards must
and the promise of drunkenness.

Packed and ready,
I listen to ghost-freight calunk
calunk through the empty station
as a breath of air
dries the sweat of dawn.
That first familiarity
with one of several billion stars,
still cherished in its ossuary of light,
now free to head West,
toward Santiago.

Another Time

Summer rain on dusty leaves
freshens dusty memories:
a manuscript, some rolled up sheaves,

smoke on hills toward the sea,
the evening light like pearl and fire,
a stranger's lilt, a rosary,

moonlight on a whinstone spire,
tombstones, yew and mistletoe:
my lives unwinding hour by hour

before a flash wipes out the show
and thunder rumbles loud reprieve,
allowing leaves to duly grow,

and me to seek repentance, grieve.

EARTH

Passing Through

Córdoba at evening,
its *calle* ramble,
beetles thrum the air.

A moon wastes
above the city's domes
and foam of the Guadalquivir.

Here, Seneca launched toy boats,
watched them capsize
beneath swirly waves

and the Caliph built *la mezquita* –
a call to Damascus –
his ear cocked for nightingales.

So far from home
living with hemlock or peppermint –
a thirst to quench;

it's been long since
musk was on these fingertips
or Lucan's sun blinded my eyes.

A traveller picks a walnut
from a plate, bites
it in two:

EARTH

click, stamp,
chords plucked on gut,
the Earth a castanet

los gritos
de los nómadas
echo down a hundred hundred years.

calle: *streets*; Guadalquivir: *river running through Córdoba*; la mezquita: *the great mosque of Córdoba*; los gritos de los nómadas: *the cries of the nomads*

Dreams

I

In the glass door
the landscape reflected.

A hill
takes my house
to China.
I fall back asleep
and realise
it's a smudge
left by a hand.

Li Po chuckles –
probably a magpie.

EARTH

II

after Jean-François Mathé

It's perhaps
the moment when I wake
that my dream
has power over the world:

just after rain
the horizon frees
a white horse that
brings me back
from afar
to my bed.

III

In the plashy half-light
I watch naked angels
dance about me in circles
dressed in gold and white.

Their braided belts and hair
fold me into bronzing air.
How wish and place conspire,
show falling rain as rising fire.

Nightmares

I

I dig to lever thistles, thorns,
turn spade on spade to fill
each hole left by the hole behind,
across and back, until the weeds
are heaped up on the fire.

Unused to graft, by nine it's bed.
I fall asleep, dig
down beneath hard rock to reach
our planet's iron core,
burn like thistles, thorns before.

II

Knock knock knock.
Get up.
Part the blind.

Clouds like buffalo
gallop
across the sky.

Knock knock. The Earth
thunders to hooves,
sidewalks rattle.

Knock. A stranger's face
bleached
in the mirror.

III

There's no elation
in the suffocation
and tearing of hair,
only despair,

as I died once more
by the crypt door
that in the Holy Book
rolled lightly back.

EARTH

Revisiting Tombs

Lucy laughing in the Theban heat:
her lips red coral, eyes like jade,
Ramses half as big as my heart
banging like a hand-grenade.

Weathermen warned it would get rough:
downpours, thunder, gale force winds.
We shrugged it off, called Tut's bluff,
made the Valley of the Kings.

That night the desert flickered white.
I watched, got drunk, discussed the chain
of chance that led us there that night
and kissed her mouth wet with rain.

Today, I walk this level sand,
remember storms that brought worse luck.
As lightning cracked from sky to land,
she proved fickle, I got struck.

wester voe

the earliest light
turquoise
the breakers
a rush
of white noise
that roll
back
the land
roll
back
the land

the rain
or is it spray?
giddies
in the swing
of Sumburgh

a runway
rides the appalling
rise and spill
of Atlantic night

from which
you lift
to leave
my blustery life
again

EARTH

not forever
I hope
although
who knows?
the rolling tide
rips any
way
even under

EARTH

The Big Witch

Singing like a girl in the sunshine
you carefully cut
the ivy's vines and claws
from a ruckle of rocks
to uncover a pit
that reveals a well – in your garden.

Like in a fairy-tale,
it is entombed, forgotten,
awaiting that true-love kiss
or those curious fingers of Pandora.

You drop a stone.
One... two... three... four... five... plop!
Your brow ripples,
as if you see an unknown face
reflected in a mirror.

Grabbing a torch,
your bent hand
shines a beam down into darkness.
The clearing of your throat
cackles back its thunderclap.

Note: In parts of France the 'Big Witch' is said to live at the bottom of water wells.

Hour in Nafplio

for Anne

Replacing an ultraviolet bulb in the pump
that cleans the water in the pond,
I remove the third screw and washer
that secures the phalange on the underside
of the upper armature
and remember Nafplio,
our view from the hostel rooftop
across the open-armed bay
as the day marooned
and small flares ignited in tavernas around the harbour
vying with a dying sun to be, briefly,
Apollo of the purple hair,
Aphrodite of the flaming sea.
Jibs stood steady
over a freighter in the docks
as they camouflaged into shadow
and hamlets once hid in the mountains
flickered orange in an asphalt sky
as if suspended
among Arcturus and Mars.
A fair-haired traveller
asked in her wiry twang, 'you guys English?'
and we laughed to think you were a guy,
which made us English
and left the blonde bemused.

EARTH

I reassemble the pump,
switch on to gurgling
then the sluice and splash of chilly water.

That was a year ago.
I had wanted to mark in words
you and me and that hour in Nafplio
for twenty years.

Roots

for Donald Adamson

Come home each passing year,
drink from the spring of childhood,
sit in the garden chair,
watch the well-kent wood,
breathe the morning atmosphere
full of gossiping rooks.

Shun the quick grass
that shoots between stones,
the orphaned hours amassed,
buzz of waxy drones
and rush of parting galaxies
that shoo you to another home.

Kim

Kim came here from Cardiff
after two failed
suicides. She is fifty;
her family disown her,
even her sons and daughter.
Kim learns the Koran
and likes keeping house.
'I luv u Kim' is painted on
Arafat's felucca.
'She needs looking after,'
he says. He's thirty,
smokes shisha, hassles tourists.
Kim wears dark glasses,
on taxi rides recites
reasons for loving Luxor.
She hopes to be a guide
to the tombs and temples
that shimmer like amber
across the choppy Nile.
The dead fascinate her.

Home Guard

She picks them from the gutter
till her pockets bulge
with shiny new-borns.
She strokes each globe.
Their weight and waxy grain comfort her,
relic of the table
that kept them safe
through huddled-under-it nights
as Heinkels whined down bombs
to rattle heart and home,
leave morning-after
smoke, soot and tears.

Like a sapper she crawls,
laying her haul by the skirting-board.
They settle in the carpet.
She's mined every room.

Spiders are bigger than ever –
it's climate change and immigration.
She has a photo
of one hairy monster, cut from *The Sun*,
ready to pounce,
as proof for passing carers
who think she's bonkers –
spiders don't like conkers.

EARTH

Each night,
like an air-raid warden
she scans the ceiling,
that unconquerable expanse of sky,
looks for a tell-tale trail,
scurry or shadow,
fears that heart-in-mouth
drop
into lap or hair,
tangle of legs and fingers,
lips pursed,
eyes pressed close

as arachnid invaders force entry
and with a Teutonic sneer
spin and suck inside her
till she withers
and dries.

The Hunter

The light is dark, anticipating thunder;
lizards pause and lick the heavy air;
a wary song thrush guards her nest from plunder;
mosquitoes dance above the wicker chair.

Behind the wood, a huntsman fires his rifle
as lightning throws its flash across the town;
vineyards glow and tremble to the rainfall
and children stop their games and run for home.

The hunter's wife comes in and hangs a rabbit,
wipes its sticky blood from off her hands,
takes another from its rusting gibbet,
chops the meat and throws it in the pan.

Rain leaks its beat upon the kitchen floor
as thunder rattles farmhouse roof and door.

After the Flood

New Orleans, June 2006

By the window, I dry off.
Laid naked below,
Big Easy awaits another storm.

Blue lights strafe Canal Street
with strip-joint candour.
Police raise cordons.
Hookers decorate doorways.
A scuffle. Arrest.

Today my laundry went AWOL,
and the waitress played hangman
with knives and spoons.
On a tour, the bus driver got lost
as a guy in a grey suit
recited from the guidebook about Desire
and we counted Chevvies
stacked under a turnpike bridge.

I try on my new shirt
from Banana Republic. As I button up,
flickers of crazy voltage
scorch the freeway, rain like smashed eggs
punches the glass. Decatur empties,
streetcars stop.

EARTH

I head for the elevator,
take the stairs,
push onto the sidewalk.
The only safe street's Bourbon,
its whorehouses lit for trade.
I drift to the Carousel.
The barman shakes a Sidecar,
says zombies have quit their tombs
and traipse the Mississippi mud,
drifting like smoke from a stale cigar
and adds, pouring my Rye,
we've only the 'gators
to keep us safe.

EARTH

The Party's Over

The cat shot out as he walked in,
the fridge went clunk and shuddered off;
left-overs choked the pedal bin
and Claret soaked the tablecloth.

'Excuse the mess' – she cleared a chair –
'would you like a cup of tea?'
He sat and preened his greying hair.
'Mine's black, no sugar, if you please.'

China chinked upon the tray;
he tapped his foot and tweaked his tie;
she asked if he was here to stay;
a damp Digestive fed a fly.

'That man in black, you saw him leave?'
Her neighbour shook his head, concerned.
She found a note: 'A brief reprieve.'
The fridge switched on, the cat returned.

EARTH

The Fall

*Take your swimming gear if you want to splash and
swim in the fresh water*
www.geocache.com on a waterfall near Köycegiz, Turkey

A pine tree's height above the pool
he stares down at his friends.
It's clear the sightless, awful fall
has drained the guts bravado lends.

And then he dives, survives the drop;
his comrades scream and hoot.
He looks to where I stand and clap
to welcome valour's new recruit.

But as I watched that afternoon
I saw this handsome boy
pinned down with his whole platoon,
mortared as it redeploys

or rigged with pounds of dynamite
at a checkpoint where
he grips his mother's photo tight
and blows infidels into air.

A Dark Place

i.m. Jeff White
poet, sculptor, thinker, friend

Sunflowers smile across the Saintonge
but I duck under
a sombre bridge
as rain comes on
in huge tears
blackening the tarmac
before a storm closes in.

If only the fizz of lightning
could tickle your toes,
spark a twinkle in your eye
and the boom of thunder
wake the dead.

EARTH

Elegy

i.m. Willy

A tractor draws the distance to a close,
defining land from overwhelming sky;
Earth is seeded to revivify:
the sun commands, the rapeseed duly grows

while you, discarded into flames, receive
the least response, last seen as soon forgot.
I read your name but who will tend the plot,
who frame the photos, log the love and grieve?

It's no great loss to leave so much unmissed,
without a tear, a verse, without a son.
Who could want the fuss when all is done?
Perhaps life's best when left unsung, unkissed.

The ploughshare parts the earth with simple grace,
its blade reflects the sun; the sun ploughs space.

Black Box

i.m. Arnot, exhibition fitter

I asked for a space
blacker than night
and you the magician
pulled one
out of your toolbox.

You flicked a switch.
We disappeared.

The sun
prodded and poked
determined to find fault or fissure
in your handiwork
to no avail.

Cheerily, you drove off
for your *boite de nuit*
and raved through the small hours,
partying the drunken darkness,
the devil's master craftsman

till Jack-in-a-box
sprung
and opened your eyes for good –
the palette-knife of morning
bloodying the East
above the road to Rennes.

boite de nuit: nightclub

A Clean Man

i.m. Ronald Thorp

He left his bed
to take a bath. At first,
a one-off, then
once or twice a week,
but soon as often as the heater
supplied hot water.

He would scrub
with brush, flannel and pumice,
scraping the skin till sore,
a little bit more
left behind each wash
as scum in tepid water.

He sat wrinkled,
coal tar soap in hand,
a few cold suds
around knobbly knees
as the nurse pulled the plug,
heaved to haul him out
then threw a towel over his corpse,
the bath-tub gurgling
as it drained.

EARTH

The Architect of Fruit

Charles Rennie Mackintosh (1868–1928)

Surveying the roads of Rousillon,
he plucks dark figs, draws blood, moves on.

A pear, a peach, each branch its load,
each tree a tracery on the road.

His tongue probes curves of soft-carved plums;
he breathes the scent of stony almonds.

His passage planned by path and plot,
he builds with walnut, apple, apricot,

elevates his projected world
through cherry, vine and lavender field

to found his hope upon dark sloes
and cap his dreams with orange groves.

Note: Scottish architect Charles Rennie Mackintosh spent his last years in Roussillon, a fruit-growing region in south-west France.

Burns' Night 2009

i.m. Adrian Mitchell (1932–2008)

Tonight the driven snow unearths the dead,
unmaps the land where Burns importuned fame
then rode in red to guarantee his bread –
much more than Truth, he chased down purse and name.

And Adrian, you'd recognise this man
with mouths to feed and pain a gnawing threat –
who wouldn't welcome such a pension plan?
As Rabbie says, *a man's a man*... and all that.

So life makes fools of men yet pays them back:
the portrait, post, committee, royal gong –
but you could never tread that beaten track,
nor advocate a path your heart deemed wrong.

A child, you trek across this fresh snow-fall,
redeeming ways we thought impassable.

EARTH

The Eastern Empire

i.m. Angus Calder (1942–2008)

Leaving the Sea of Marmara
your cargo skirts the coastline, chugs
behind Theodosius' wall and berths
along the glitzy Bosphorus.

My Toll Cross Horace – worthy tag:
haranguer, scholar, poet, chum,
sharp as flint and kind as soap,
you deserve this bright Byzantium.

You'll lord it, friend to goldsmiths,
jewelled whores, saints and clowns;
you'll prick a capital's soiled conscience,
play vizier and cracker of crowns...

but journeys end oddly, old ghost:
I foresee your ship set sail, float free
above palaces, minarets,
trailing phosphor bound for the Black Sea.

Note: I was in Istanbul when I heard the news, through a chance encounter, of Angus Calder's rapidly declining health.

Encounters

It is time to enquire thy fate
Virgil, Aeneid, VI

I

It takes so long to say goodbye.
I'm on a boat that skirts the coast
over an oily sea;
the sun is all blue sky
and friends wear champagne toasts
towards evening.

Making port, shadows gather,
among them my father –
frail but *Ben n Light* in mood.
Like gurgling springs
our laughter wells up and sings.
I've never grinned so broad.

He's as I knew him years ago,
the man who bounced me on his knee.
We hold a long embrace.
'Stay here,' he says
and I, 'But Dad, you know…'
then pull my shoulders free.

EARTH

II

We legged it from port following
dusty tracks that climbed to hills.
Moving among olive trees –
voices; in the houses, cracked
like broken teeth in rotten gums –
ghosts. I'm afraid of ambush.
My mates seem careless as lambs
but I see footprints, signals
that belong to neon streets –
men that wear Hush-Puppies,
ties and braces, angry scowls;
women with lips like poppies,
parading their tango, fox-trot;
kids hungry for gold; fighters
and cowards, victims of bombs
and booze, sad and bitter, lost.

EARTH

III

The air is clammy and the stars are hot;
we sit around the fire swatting flies.
Some tell stories. I talk of how I met
my father at the port. My neighbour shivers,
haunted by silent movies from his past.
We realise, one by one, this is why
we're here, chasing ghosts among cypresses.
We toast our fate with warm wine from the Co
then sleep, and dream of what we wouldn't know.

IV

You look at me, eye to eye,
and say you failed, you too.
You, who signed your masterwork
at the age I reach today,
you who made silence sing,
account yourself a loss and worse
than Gilbert, cooker of books,
who dressed his ghosts as truths,
or Ron whose life passed on the Post.
Where are you leading me?
Why this hilltop hamlet in Tuscany,
with fat tourists by the pool
and spiders in their tawdry webs?
Each time I stop, you push me on.
Eyes blink behind windows.
You shift among the mazy streets,
towers, gardens, horseflies, heat
and slick lizards. I pluck a fig,
hear a shadow whisper, 'thief!'
'Liar,' shouts a skirt that slips
around a wall, down an alley.
'Failure,' calls a blond boy
from a terraced olive grove.
You take me to a man who blends
shadow and sun, sun and stone,
stone and foliage, foliage and fire,
fire and rain, then lead me back
to camp, among the dreaming.

EARTH

V

I'm on a boat
upon the Thames
leaving the sea.
Ethereal blue
reaches through
the starboard window.
My father, no
longer luminous,
knows that I
must make for land
and leave. We drink
a beer. Others
sit too near.

We up and look
each into
the others' eyes.
Tears wash away
his ghost until
only sunlight's
left and I
walk onto
Greenwich jetty.

EARTH

The Widows of Vathia

Our homes rise from rock
        block on block
                over promontory and sea
we lurk in cloaked rooms
                dressed in black
                      shutters frame our gaze
    our endless gaze
                    nothing escapes us
tourists wander paths and steps
        duck beneath lintels
                and dissolve
we are cursed with sight
            hindsight
                    foresight
we collect
    its left-overs
        goat droppings
                      the endless fire
            that beaconed Priam's death
    screams of men
        sheep bleating on hillsides
                summer flies
our sons have gone to wars
        all dead, I think
            for sure, all dead
our husbands
    what of them?
        gone
                gone

EARTH

    each man and child
                                       shall we name them all?
                    gone
                                gone
        each pet name
                                        recalled
                    each endearment
      felt
                        each coat
          without shoulders on which to hang
     as the world unbuckles
         undoes
                unclothes
                              unseams
unseemly
       we call to them
                        and cry
                             cry for the end
          now

we drift in space
                          and drift
       even after Earth's final flame
             after the sun is spent
                         the last widows
         in starless dark
dried hags
              sisters in this stony tomb
        typical, cold.

Note: Vathia is an ancient hilltop village in the south of the Mani peninsula on the Greek Peloponnesus.

EARTH

Mimicking Icarus

I

As a kid, I played,
arms wide,
flying a Phantom,
tail on fire,
spiralling
a plume of smoke
towards the streets
till I crashed
on my back
the world giddy,
even with eyes
tight closed.

EARTH

II

Today it's oohs and ahs
from the viewing platform
but that's a long fall in flames,
to ricochets of screams
and smoke across Manhattan –
concrete made of dreams,
by nightmares flattened.

III

Five miles high,
the moon pastes cloud below.

I'll not break silence
but navigate by Pegasus' stars,
fly up,
giddy the altimeter,
merge with remote space,
renounce my clay.

How many men suffer to sail
the sky, their last music,
breathless air,
their last vision, a marble Earth?

EARTH

House on the Lagoon

I

This evening water's high.
The trees that mark its margins
sink, the jetties and holiday homes
sprayed with the spume
of wind-blown lagoon.

I shutter the windows,
keep the light for me,
hope evil passes by.
I guess at the earth's motion:
a wind-buffet,
splash, a gurgle, clank.

Beneath my dreams, rain drums,
the slurp and slap of restless water
knocks at my floor,
seeps through the tongue and groove,
soaks my slippers.

Come morning I welcome the maid
splish-splashing on boards
like one who walks on water.

EARTH

II

When the water's still
graceful jellyfish pulse like ballerinas
around igneous rocks. They feed
on creatures so small
only Caribbean sun
reveals their innocent specks.

At night
these diaphanous medusas
shoal beneath my bedroom
black as a bad bruise
their tentacles spooling
on stanchions and barnacles.

When the east wind
shimmies the lagoon's glib surface,
all swarms below are hid
and the lip-lapping
of wavelets, like benign laughter,
amuses the ear.

Settings

I

The hunter prone –
smashed on rum.
Even his dog looks dosey.

Fish peck at his toes,
eels wrap his legs,
drag him down
to drown and be gorged upon
by creatures
that never even bleeped
as hostiles
on his radar.

II

As she falls into the lake
a puff of smoke.

III

Sail, engine, oars
defy the current
so untie the mooring,
let the boat drift,
the tiller raised...

Routes

I leave by a different route
that seems the same
as the one I came by.

The fox has bright ideas
about a to b.
My headlights spark his eyes.

EARTH

London back streets –
all bollarded now.
My car wants a way home.

The sat-nav insists right.
I go straight on,
arrive home after all.

Snow covers tracks
then tracks of tracks.
Any way will do.

EARTH

Crossing

Riverlap and sweet mimosa
fill the midnight air of Africa.

I lurch aboard; the anchor strains;
a creak of wood and clash of chains.

The engine smokes its diesel growl
and night responds with monkey howls.

Orion swings a half way round,
and thud, the ferry runs aground.

I stand alone, expectant lover,
then kneel to kiss this terra nova.

Love Story

We speculate on how we might live
upon the moon; unfooled
by a poet's wistfulness, we know
dead rock, guess at what it is
to suffocate, feel our blood boil
as moon-cold seizes our marrow.

A staging-post on a journey, I say;
What journey? Where? you ask,
and the deadliness of space,
its forever footprints and betrayals,
unfolds like a Romance
with an unforeseen ending.

'Love' a poet once said,
'is a sign of evolution.'
Is this paramour's pebble,
thrown at our window every night,
here to charm or remind us
that love's a Cyclops, not blind?

EARTH

Eye to Eye

for Lesley

Somewhere, perhaps, far away on an Earth
circling an alien star, a man stares across
the night. He studies heaven for signs of breath
disturbing cosmic dust like wind on floss.

Elsewhere, a woman, one million parsecs out
inhabits an oasis bathed in air.
She looks for patterns in condensing clouds
of gas that indicate life may live there.

Today, the sunrise animates our house.
You pick a dress, ask *if…* and I reply
of course, and you *but why?* and me *who knows?*
our thanks for every day passed eye to eye.

EARTH

The Art of the Pond

There's no arguing with water.
It will do its will. You cannot command it
go up hill, nor make its surface
other than an horizon.

Friends come round for a drink.
I sit there and say:
*I dug the hole,
the water, chuckling,
took up residence.*

It went its way
as ponds do
despite my stones and channels,
polythene and pipes

but those unchristened
into the way of water
gloat. Advice comes in waves.

My last ditch last word to them:
*A pond builds itself.
Just go with the flow.*

Clearances

On the news
Etna's spewing;
down the alley
Venus dances in a puddle.

Weed strung
over a canal's elbow
like a wedding train.

EARTH

In the yard
sun on yellow sandstone
lapping like the ocean.

Filming, the moon's
absent. Reviewing,
a TV sprays with stars.

EARTH

Systems' failure.
New code finds room.

A jet unzips the sky.
Air flaps loose
then
pulls itself together.

EARTH

First gear bend:
cloud and moor
shift sunlight.

Rain
drips
past
the
door,
cleans
the
step.

harbour seal

among this morning's slate-greys
a seal sliding under
a see-through sea

head up
buoy bobbing?
before roll
flip
dappled hide
and forked tail
dive

beneath
a quick squall's glare
of grey wavelets

(a short sheen of
whiskers,
an eye-blink)

then the pull
of cliffs
skerries
mackerel shoals
the slate-grey Atlantic

EARTH

a tidal belonging
elsewhere

leaves
slate-grey emptiness.

EARTH

light-hearted on burra

the world's big
up here

and gets bigger
as day
closes down

lights switch on

at first from boats
rolling ocean's back
then cars
that scutter
over islands
home

then planets
stars

then
fainter
galaxies
leaping from might be
into sidelong
sight

EARTH

only then
beyond
the hissing quasars
is there
lightlessness

that lurks
in mirrors
handshakes
laughter

the dazzling darkness
into which
we will
be made

The Pelican

A pelican and I sit out a storm.
It preens as lightning cracks on scrub.
We share patience; rain unites.

A clearing in the east, a last
thunderclap and, sure enough,
the pelican flies off to scoop shoaling fish.

I also head for sea – that reservoir
of tears – renouncing reflection
for a dip in waves of bitter fulfilment.

The Frog

A blackbird launches its evening lyric
(nightingales hold off
till moonrise silvers the scene)

You call me indoors
to watch a stray grasshopper hop,
cup it in your hands
then go outside to set it down,
free, on the patio,
only for the biggest frog I have ever seen
to leap like a ballerina from the undergrowth and snap!
swallow it with a crunch
then lope away.

I have spent my life reading poems
and realise, tonight, for the first time,
that I haven't understood a single one –
not one.

The spruce
that stood out so boldly all winter
is now quite lost
among the greens of the oak woods.

Suddenly a nightingale
sings the world to ash.

In the Garden

I hanker after figs,
pluck handfuls from heavy branches,
juggle them hot as coals

to the kitchen. Teeth slice
flesh erupting molten cores,
lava pours down my fingers.

I gorge on stars,
chew cinders and fire,
blown away by the Big Bang's budding.

Earth 2.0

I'm dressing a crab for supper
when I hear on the BBC
a newly discovered planet,
Kepler 22-b, an Earth-type body
six hundred light years far, a year
of two hundred and ninety days
and an ambient warmth like
the Canaries in winter, is circling
its somewhat sickly sun. Scientists
speculate about oceans of H2O,
breathable atmosphere, acids,
bacteria, algae, fish, mammals,
the mirror-glance of *how's my lipstick?*,
civilization, technology and TV.
My crab looks sadly up at me.
Its legs lie strewn on the counter.
Suddenly I feel lonely this night
and am struck that we will die,
all of us and every living thing,
everywhere; the Earth's days
numbered. This long journey,
on which the crab and I crawl –
though it walked sideways
and I uphill, while others sit still –
must end. And all Earths, no
matter where, no matter what sun
holds them in its arms, no matter
what hurts, hopes and hallelujahs,
have ended or will end. There is no fairy-
tale prince, no star-dust to make us

EARTH

forever smile, no up with the lark
when the sun don't rise. All memories,
dreams, grumbles, laughter, building,
comfort, myth-making, birth,
prayer, love, rambles, poems,
gardening, supper, tears, goodnights,
phone-calls, kisses, heaven
end in one leave-taking, one blink,
and are gone, utterly, and time, dead.

More poetry from Luath press

The Luath Kilmarnock Edition: Poems Chiefly in the Scottish Dialect
Robert Burns
ISBN: 978-1-906307-67-7 HBK £15

Merry Muses of Caledonia
Robert Burns
ISBN: 978-1-906307-68-4 HBK £15

Scunnered
Des Dillon
ISBN: 978-1-908373-04-5 PBK £6.99

Dancing with Big Eunice
Alistair Findlay
ISBN: 978-1-906817-28-2 PBK £7.99

The Love Songs of John Knox
Alistair Findlay
ISBN: 978-1-905222-30-8 PBK £7.99

Never Mind the Captions
Alistair Findlay
ISBN: 978-1-906817-89-3 PBK £7.99

Shale Voices
Alistair Findlay
ISBN: 978-1-906307-11-0 PBK £10.99

Kate o Shanter's Tale
Matthew Fitt
ISBN: 978-1-842820-28-5 PBK £6.99

Jane: Poems of a Performance Poet
Anita Govan
ISBN: 978-1-905222-14-8 PBK £6.99

Blind Ossian's Fingal
James Macpherson
ISBN: 978-1-906817-55-8 HBK £15

Love and Revolution
Alastair Mcintosh
ISBN: 978-1-905222-58-2 PBK £8.99

Burning Whins
Liz Niven
ISBN: 978-1-842820-74-2 PBK £8.99

Stravaigin
Liz Niven
ISBN: 978-1-905222-70-4 PBK £7.99

Bad Ass Raindrop
Kokumo Rocks
ISBN: 978-1-842820-18-6 PBK £6.99

Stolen from Africa
Kokumo Rocks
ISBN: 978-1-906307-19-6 PBK £7.99

Bodywork
Dilys Rose
ISBN: 978-1-905222-93-3 PBK £8.99

A Long Stride Shortens the Road
Donald Smith
ISBN: 978-1-842820-73-5 PBK £8.99

Into the Blue Wavelengths
Roderick Watson
ISBN: 978-1-842820-75-9 PBK £8.99

Bunnets 'n' Bowlers
Brian Whittingham
ISBN: 978-1-906307-94-3 PBK £8.99

Drink the Green Fairy
Brian Whittingham
ISBN: 978-1-842820-45-2 PBK £8.99

Accent o the Mind
Rab Wilson
ISBN: 978-1-905222-32-2 PBK £8.99

Life Sentence
Rab Wilson
ISBN: 978-1-906307-89-9 PBK £8.99

A Map for the Blind
Rab Wilson
ISBN: 978-1-906817-82-4 PBK £8.99

The Ruba'iyat of Omar Kayyam in Scots
Rab Wilson
ISBN: 978-1-842820-46-9 PBK £8.99

Details of these and other books published by Luath Press can be found at:
www.luath.co.uk

Luath Press Limited
committed to publishing well written books worth reading

LUATH PRESS takes its name from Robert Burns, whose little collie Luath (*Gael.,* swift or nimble) tripped up Jean Armour at a wedding and gave him the chance to speak to the woman who was to be his wife and the abiding love of his life. Burns called one of 'The Twa Dogs' Luath after Cuchullin's hunting dog in Ossian's *Fingal*. Luath Press was established in 1981 in the heart of Burns country, and is now based a few steps up the road from Burns' first lodgings on Edinburgh's Royal Mile.
Luath offers you distinctive writing with a hint of unexpected pleasures.

Most bookshops in the UK, the US, Canada, Australia, New Zealand and parts of Europe either carry our books in stock or can order them for you. To order direct from us, please send a £sterling cheque, postal order, international money order or your credit card details (number, address of cardholder and expiry date) to us at the address below. Please add post and packing as follows: UK – £1.00 per delivery address; overseas surface mail – £2.50 per delivery address; overseas airmail – £3.50 for the first book to each delivery address, plus £1.00 for each additional book by airmail to the same address. If your order is a gift, we will happily enclose your card or message at no extra charge.

Luath Press Limited
543/2 Castlehill
The Royal Mile
Edinburgh EH1 2ND
Scotland
Telephone: 0131 225 4326 (24 hours)
Fax: 0131 225 4324
email: sales@luath.co.uk
Website: www.luath.co.uk

Printed by RR Donnelley at Glasgow, UK